The One Minute President!

The Quickest Way To Advance Your Own Political Agenda
And Still Have Everyone Think You're A Hell Of A Nice Guy

Paul Fericano, Ph.D.
Elio Ligi, D.D., D.D.S.

POOR SOULS BOOKS
YOSSARIAN UNIVERSAL NEWS SERVICE

MILLBRAE • PORTLAND • LONDON • BEIRUT

This Poor Souls Book contains the complete text of the original manuscript.

THE ONE MINUTE PRESIDENT

A Poor Souls Book / published by special arrangement with
The Portland Pataphysical Outpatient Clinic, Lounge and Laundromat.

Poor Souls Press is a wholly owned subsidiary of
YOSSARIAN UNIVERSAL (YU) NEWS SERVICE.

PRINTING HISTORY
Poor Souls Trade paperback edition / February 1987
Second printing / March 1987

For information write:
Yossarian Universal News Service • P.O. Box 236
Millbrae • CA • 94030 • USA

ISBN: 0-916296-10-5

One Minute Wishes: Recapitulation contains material from "Young At Heart" (© 1954; Words: Caroline Leigh; Music: Johnny Richards) from the film *Young At Heart*.

One Minute Retaliations: Recapitulation contains material from "When You Wish Upon A Star" (© 1940; Words: Ned Washington; Music: Leigh Harline) from the film *Pinnochio*.

Why One Minute Retaliations Work contains four lines from William Collins' "Ode Written In the Year 1746."

Whale icon by Jean Liji; Cover collage by Dr. Alfred J. Faustroll

PRINTED IN THE UNITED STATES OF AMERICA

For Clint Eastwood

Wooden-headedness, the source of self-deception, is a factor that plays a remarkably large role in government. It consists in assessing a situation in terms of preconceived fixed notions while ignoring or rejecting any contrary signs. It is acting according to wish while not allowing oneself to be deflected by the facts. It is epitomized in a historian's statement about Philip II of Spain, the surpassing woodenhead of all sovereigns: "No experience of the failure of his policy could shake his belief in its essential excellence."

— Barbara W. Tuchman,
The March of Folly

 Introduction

IN EARLY 1984, two American satirists decided to take on the burgeoning **One Minute Industry** by lampooning the **One Minute Method**'s most regal example: the President of the United States. Their efforts were not widely applauded.

The original manuscript, completed in May, 1984, was rejected by more than two dozen American publishers before being purchased by Stroessner, Schultz, and Rilke (Munich), which, as it turns out, was a CIA front operation.

Manuscript versions of the work have circulated internationally for several years, and the book has garnered laudatory reviews in such forums as **Krokodil, La Prensa, Ash Shiraa,** and **Inside Joke.** In fact, **The One Minute President** is now required reading at several prestigious universities, including American University (Beirut) and Moscow University (Idaho).

YOSSARIAN UNIVERSAL NEWS SERVICE feels it is time for the Amcrican people to have equal opportunity to master the management style the President feels has served him so well.

The **One Minute President** is not merely the stinging indictment of a system of government and thought so bereft of meaning and morality that even whales beach themselves on our shores to protest it.

No, it is much more than that. While we realize that the ideas and precepts embodied in these pages will never gain as wide an audience as the Pentateuch, we do believe that each and every American can benefit from the concepts that make up the **One Minute Philosophy**.

Now, more than ever, Americans need such knowledge and guidance to protect them from this awesome truth: *Anybody can grow up to be President.*

And that means not only you, but that maniac across the street.

This book is for those who would pursue the Presidential dream.

We are convinced you will enjoy implementing what you learn from the **One Minute President** and that, as a consequence, you and the people who will vote and die for you will enjoy merrier, less stressful, and more economically feasible lives.

Paul Fericano, Ph.D.
Elio Ligi, D.D., D.D.S.

 Contents

ONCE THERE WAS an ambitious young man who was looking for an effective President.

His quest had taken him over many years to the numb reaches of the universe.

He had been in the smallest of bombed-out hamlets and in the graffiti-plastered megalopolises of wealthy nations.

He had spoken with many leaders and had begun to see the entire color wheel of how Presidents could be loved by the very people they annihilated.

He had come across many "honorable" Presidents whose countries seemed to win while their people died by the thousands of hunger, poison, and disease.

As the young man sat in the offices of each of these Presidents, he usually asked: "So what kind of President would you say you are?"

Their answers varied only slightly.

"I am not a crook," or "I can't remember," he was told.

He also met many "space-cadet" Presidents, whose people seemed to be doing okay, while their neighbors died by the thousands of hunger, poison, and disease. As the young man drank white wine and listened to *these* Presidents answer the same question, he heard this:

"Relax and let go. Just manage your stress. Then everything's under control."

After awhile, it seemed to him that most Presidents were only interested in getting away with as much as they could before they got caught, or appearing as though they were getting away with nothing when they were, in fact, getting away with it all.

Of course, there were some who were trying to pass themselves off as effective Presidents, even going so far as to have extensive cosmetic surgery to correct certain deficiencies in their public image. But they didn't fool anyone. In fact, people enjoyed laughing at these Presidents and just plain liked having them around.

In time, the young man began seriously to doubt he would ever find an effective President. "How can one man," he wondered, "be expected to change his mind every day on both crucial and trivial decisions, confuse the intent, misdirect the purpose and still achieve a maximum of incompetent effectiveness?"

The young man shook his head. "Perhaps," he thought, "I am asking for too much."

Deeply disturbed and disappointed, he considered a life of drug abuse and degradation. And he would have pursued it too, had he not felt a strange, whiny voice within urging him to say "No!" to despair and continue his search for an effective President.

THEN ONE DAY, he began hearing wonderful and witty stories about a special President who lived, appropriately enough, in another world.

He heard that people were actually sincere in their affections toward this President, accepting whatever he said or did with an overwhelming wave of respect, especially when what he said or did nearly always contradicted whatever he had previously said or done.

In truth, this President's point of persuasion was so complete, that just about everyone had something nice to say about him, yet no one could remember why.

The young man also heard some fascinating stories about how this President had implemented new guidelines that simplified communication. People were encouraged to engage in repetitious and monotonous discussions of issues and events that had very little to do with intelligent thinking. People were genuinely proud of what they didn't know, and they demonstrated this again and again by eagerly opposing everything by simply approving the opposite of what they already didn't understand.

"This might be just the President I've been looking for," thought the young man. But he wondered if these stories were really true.

There was only one way to find out.

"I'd like to make an appointment to meet with the President," he told the special secretary who screened his call.

"Fine," said the secretary. "Just check your weapons at the front gate and drop by any time."

When the young man arrived at the President's office he found several other men milling around outside. He spotted a secretary's desk and approached her. "Hello. I'm here to see the President," he announced.

"Good for you," she said, without looking up, "Go right in."

"But what about these other gentlemen?" He asked, amazed at how casual the procedure was. "Aren't they ahead of me?"

"Don't be ridiculous," she said. "They're on duty."

As the young man opened the door to the President's office, a spry and enthusiastic President bounded across the room and vigorously shook the young man's hand.

"Come in, come in," the President smiled, "I've been expecting you."

"You have?"

"Haven't I?"

The young man took an immediate fancy to this President. And he was impressed with his office, too. Except for a sofa-chair that appeared bolted to the floor in the middle of the room, a podium facing the chair, and an enormous video screen that took up the entire wall behind the podium, the office was completely empty and the walls entirely bare.

There was no desk to lose things on. No bookcases stocked with books no one had ever read. No historical paintings of questionable leaders to gaze at and become inspired by. And no long, tasteless drapes to tug at and fuss over.

In fact, there were no windows, either.

It was, without question, the most efficiently clutter-less office the young man had ever been in, and he marvelled at such genius.

The President, still smiling and clasping the young man's hand, invited him to sit down in the sofa-chair while he took his own place behind the podium.

"So," the President grinned, "Where were we?"

The young man quickly glanced around the room, but they were completely alone. He looked back at the President who was still grinning, waiting for a reply.

"Oh! Well, actually," the young man blushed, clearing his throat, "The reason I'm here is I heard you were an effective President and, quite frankly, that's what I hope to be someday."

"Good answer," congratulated the President. "But what does that have to do with me?"

"Well, if what I've been hearing is true, I'd like to learn your methods of governing people and hopefully get some answers to a great many questions that have been troubling me for as long as I can remember."

"Really? Well, I'm going to make sure you get every opportunity to continue doing so," assured the President.

"That's swell!" beamed the excited young man.

"I'm sure it sure is," the President agreed. "When action is required to preserve what rightfully doesn't belong to us, we will act."

"We will?"

"We won't? Then, why not?"

"Is this a test?"

"Are you talking to me?" the President yawned.

The young man loosened his tie and opened his notebook. "OK," he said, "Let me begin by asking you how you go about setting policy?"

"I don't."

"I beg your pardon?"

"That's quite all right."

"But if you don't set policy, who does?" quizzed the young man.

"Damned if I know," the President smiled. "Policy has a way of setting itself around here these days. I don't think it has anything to do with me, really, but I could be wrong."

"That's incredible, isn't it?"

"*I* don't think so," said the President. "But don't get me wrong. Occasionally, old friends drop by for a chat and we'll talk turkey. Usually, I stand here and try to listen while they sit where you are and try to analyze whatever it is they think I might have known," he explained. "But sometimes, just to see if it works, we exchange places and go through the whole process in reverse, all the while mapping out strategies and re-hearsing facial expressions. Sometimes we practice the Heimlich maneuver. Sometimes we play charades. Other times we skip the formalities and take off our shirts."

"And after that?" asked the young man, feverishly scribbling notes.

"After that," the President continued, "I usually end with a prayer asking God for wisdom and guidance, and that always gets a good laugh." And he chuckled.

"Fascinating," said the young man, licking the tip of his pencil. "And what about final decisions?"

"What about them?"

"Well, for one, are they mutually binding?"

"I certainly hope not," answered the President. "After all, what is a decision? It's just a word. And what's a word? It's something you look up in the dictionary when you can't remember how it's spelled or what its meaning is. That's no way to run a government."

"I had no idea," the young man admitted.

"And it's just as well," said the President, "because under my administration, I encourage the free exchange of notions, not ideas. And the greater the notion, the greater the flexibility with regards to changing your mind without informing or upsetting anyone beforehand. After all, it's not the idea of how we get wherever we are going that matters, but rather the all-important notion of simply getting there."

"I see," nodded the young man.

"Probably not," assured the President, "But that's not important. What is important is to not be distracted by the truth of ideas, but to be more attentive to the interpretation of the notions they camouflage. This shift creates endless possibilities when the interpretations are left open to interpretation. It gives people the added luxury of filling in the blanks, so to speak."

"I see," the young man pondered, "But how does this all work towards effectively governing people?"

"Image!" the President exclaimed. "Just take in everything I tell you and project back onto me whatever image you find appealing. Believe me, it works. And what's more, the script doesn't have to make sense to anyone but me."

"What script?"

The President chuckled. "The remaking of reality is no mistake, young man, far from it. It's a stroke of political genius."

"You're going too fast for me," the young man confessed.

"Well, good, good," said the President, much relieved. "For a minute there, I thought I was getting through to you."

The young man scratched his head. "So what is the purpose of your administration?"

"I already told you," he said.

"You did?"

"Are you saying I didn't?"

"No," the young man admitted, "but are you sure I was here?"

"Interesting concept," the President said. He paused for a moment, then asked, "Have you ever been to a circus?"

"Why, sure, but..."

"And were you sometimes afraid of the clowns?"

"Well, come to think of it, I guess I was, but..."

"So you can see my point, then," the President winked.

"Where?" and the young man's eyes darted around the room.

"Christ!" screamed the President, tearing off his toupee. "And you want to be *President* someday? Have you no eyes?" He walked out from behind the podium, reached into his pocket and produced a tiny device.

"Now pay attention to the screen," he commanded, "I flash this up there several times a day to remind me of something that escapes me at the moment."

He clicked the gadget and a buzzer went off, illuminating the screen.

People Who Think

The Government Works

For Them

Should Get A Job

As the young man stared up at the giant screen with its billboard-quality pronouncement in ten-foot high letters, the President resumed his place behind the podium and clicked off the remote-control.

"Now, let's think about people for a moment," said the President and he frowned. "Actually, people have a peculiar way of clouding one's perception of people, but forget that. For now, think about what people want from a political system. Would you say they want less government, or more?"

"Is this a trick question?"

"Good guess, but the answer is *less* government. And why do you think they want less government?"

"Because it's less filling?" the young man offered, forgetting for the moment where he was.

"No, because the notion of less government—my notion—is so much more appealing. 'Than what?' you might ask. But your neighbors would only hoot you down. And as a result, the continuous repetition of my notion only advances the opposite by direct action," and the President learned forward and smiled. "You get it?"

The young man's face lit up as though he had just tested negative. "You mean," he wagered, "telling people they want less government is a direct and purposeful link to giving them *more* government?"

"Precisely," said a satisfied President. "It's all in how you interpret my notion of less government. In fact, this particular notion works so well that in a few years, if practiced faithfully, there could be so much more 'less government' for the people to want that many will begin to feel that they have no government at all. Now *that's* something to chew on," said the President as he started on his tongue.

"But why go through all this backdoor maneuvering?" questioned the young man. "Why not use the same method and tell the people exactly what they're going to get?"

"Look," explained the President. "You don't go rounding up the herd by asking their permission, and you certainly don't barbecue the beef by setting fire to the range."

The young man sat there in silence, pondering all that he had heard. And although he was convinced he was in the presence of a great mind, a brilliant communicator, and an all-around neat guy, he simply couldn't, for the life of him, explain how it was possible to be so convinced. "It is clear," he thought to himself, "that I need more convincing."

The President, sensing the young man's dilemma, was moved. He walked over to one of the blank walls and said, "Come over here, young man."

He pointed to a small patch on the wall where the paint had cracked and peeled, and asked, "Do you see how the paint in this one spot has cracked and peeled?"

The young man had to look very hard to see it, and said, "It's barely noticeable."

"True," he said, "But that's not the point. The point is, it's there. And I notice it every single day I walk into this office. Sometimes, I spend hours standing in this very spot, staring at it and thinking about what it means."

"What it means?"

"Absolutely," continued the President. "I became obsessed with the idea of what this one, tiny, ugly patch of peeling paint was trying to convey."

"I don't get it," said the young man, scrutinizing the spot.

"Neither did I, at first. Then, one day, I made a startling discovery."

"Did you?"

"Yes. I discovered that this entire office had been painted by union labor."

"I see," said the young man who had never held a paint brush in his life. "Maybe a little spackle here and there might…"

"No, no, you're missing the point," the President admonished. "Think about it," he emphasized, "*Union labor.*"

The young man did think about it. "Union labor, union labor," he repeated several times, staring at the spot, mesmerized by the words. "Well, now that you mention it, I suppose there *is* a degree of principle at stake here, but…"

"No 'buts' about it," the President stressed. "*This* wall is making a statement about the structure of the work ethic in this country."

"It's a symbol, then?"

"More an omen."

"Ah, the final conflict," nodded the young man.

"And it's just such attention to detail that helps change the way I perceive the real world. The responsibility sometimes confounds even me."

"Imagine," the young man tried to imagine.

"How true," the President sighed, "How very true."

The President continued staring at the wall, deep in his own thoughts. He was remembering a time when a nickel could buy enough food and liquor to feed and stupefy a family of four for an entire month. But those days were gone forever, and he was glad they were. It astounded and delighted him to know just how far his country had come since then.

"You know," The young man said, interrupting the President's musing, "I'm reminded of a Swedish film I once saw. In it, a partially nude woman is being tied to a…"

"Yes, yes," the President said softly. "Of course she is."

He walked back to the podium, motioning for the young man to sit back down in the sofa-chair. "Let's face it," said the President. "Like it or not, no President can run a government without people hanging around long enough for him to govern. The fewer people to govern, naturally, the better, but one learns to make the right adjustments to keep the census people baffled. Still, for me, one thing remains absolutely certain."

"Death?"

"Not yet."

"Taxes?"

"Watch your language, young man."

"So what is it, then?" the young man asked in exasperation. "What are you so certain about?"

"Can't you tell?" said the President, striking a pose. "It's the kind of President I am. Or didn't you notice?"

"Notice what?"

"That I'm a **One Minute President**, of course."

"Of course," the young man agreed, not knowing what he was agreeing with, "But, if you don't mind me asking, what does that mean?"

"It simply means," said the President, leaning forward, "that it takes practically no time at all to get everything I want without bothering with national referendums, constitutional law, Senate subcommittee investigations, or scientific inquiry into why ozone is being depleted."

And for the first time, the young man eyed the President suspiciously.

"I can see you don't believe me," the President challenged.

"Oh, no, it's not that," the young man lied, "It's just that..."

"You find it difficult to swallow that I'm a **One Minute President**," the President continued.

"Well, no, but maybe I missed something," the young man confessed, thumbing through his notes. "Could we start again, perhaps?"

The President laughed. "You'd be much better off," he said, "if you spoke to some of my people first and had them tell you what kind of President I am."

"Yes, yes, I think you're right," said the young man. "Any suggestions?"

The President smiled slyly. He reached down behind the podium, produced a bulky directory, and tossed it to the young man. "What you have there is a comprehensive listing of the names, positions, phone numbers and Swiss bank accounts of over half-a-million people in my employ, including staff, cabinet members, appointees, political allies, corporate power-brokers, criminal masterminds, and so on—all close personal friends, I might add."

"This is overwhelming," said the startled young man, rifling through the directory.

"And it's updated every week," added the President.

"But where do I begin?"

"Try page one. I understand that's a very good place to begin a book."

"I mean who should I see first?"

"Talk to all of them, if you want. It makes no difference to me."

"But how do I figure this out?" The young man was beginning to panic.

"That's up to you."

"Hey, be fair," he whined. "Can't you at least give me a clue?"

"Get your ass out of that chair!" the President screamed. "Now!" And he rushed the young man, hurrying him toward the door. "What the hell do you want, young man? A road map? A guided tour? A free meal ticket? A round-trip fare? Maybe a goddamn paid vacation, is that it?"

The young man was so terrified now he couldn't speak.

"I've just about had enough of this wimpish attitude," the President continued, "You've asked me to repeat myself several times today, and, quite frankly, that galls me no end! Either you stop all this pissing and moaning and get on with it, or I'm going to take your silly search for an effective presidency and show it the dark side of the moon. Do we understand each other?"

Still speechless, the young man barely nodded as he felt his legs go numb.

Then, with an unexpected and sudden warmth the young man had only seen on certain TV shows, the President seemed to relax as he smiled and said: "But, for the moment, let's put all this aside and let me stress how impressed I am by your willingness to learn all you can about governing people, and let there be no doubt: If for some reason you still don't grasp the fundamentals after speaking with some of my people, I want you to feel free to come traipsing through this door and put your hard questions to me." And for the second time that day, he vigorously shook the young man's hand.

"I, uh, well," murmured the young man, still in shock.

"Oh, I know, I know," the President laughed opening the door and putting his arm around the young man's shoulder, "I may not give you the answers you expect to hear, and I surely won't say anything I don't want to hear myself. But you can bet I will give you answers that may prove useful if you should ever find yourself under cross-examination. And who knows?" he mused, slapping the young man on the back and propelling him out the door, "Maybe I'll even feel generous enough to give you the complete concept of the **One Minute President,** just to get you out of my hair," and he winked. "In the meantime, good luck, goodbye, and good riddance."

Then he slammed the door.

For a brief moment, the young man stood in silence, staring at the door. He felt his knees buckle. "Thank you," he managed to mumble to himself.

And then he passed out.

HERE, DRINK THIS," he heard a voice say. "It's good for you."

"What is it?" he asked, as he took a sip.

"Classic Coke," the **One Minute President**'s secretary replied.

After the young man was finally able to sit up, he apologized for falling face-first onto the secretary's IBM PC.

"That's OK," she said. "It happens all the time." Then she paused a moment before saying, "Look, I hope you don't mind, but I took the liberty of phoning all the people who work for the President to make your decision a bit easier."

The young man was dumbfounded. "You called over half a million people while I was out?"

"I'm a **One Minute Secretary**," she explained, "But it certainly doesn't hurt to have a phone with one-touch memory dialing.

"Anyway," she continued, "here's the breakdown: One-third of the people flatly refuse to talk to you, another third are out of the country, and of the remaining third, several thousand are either too busy, too sick, or too worried to talk. That leaves only a few hundred. Of those, about a third are presently under indictment, another third are already serving time, and the rest are dead."

"So who's left to talk to?"

"Six people," she said. "But three want cash up front for their time."

"And?" the young man said, a bit wearily.

"Here are the other three," and she handed him a small scrap of paper.

The young man thanked her and glanced at the names: Mr. Money, Mr. Ooze and Mrs. Bierfurter.

WHEN THE YOUNG MAN ARRIVED at Money's office, he found a slender man in a three piece pin-striped suit several sizes too large galloping around the room on a hobby horse. "Giddy-yap!" Money urged, shaking the reins furiously. Money wore oversized glasses, and as he turned to smile at his visitor, the young man half-expected to be greeted with a mouthful of braces. He seemed like a little boy dressed in his father's old clothes.

"Well," Money grinned, bringing his broomstick mount to a halt near the door, "So you've been to see the old coot, have you? Hell of a nice guy, don't you think?"

"Nicest guy you'd ever want to meet," the young man agreed.

"Told you all about being a **One Minute President,** did he?"

"Over and over," the young man replied, "But no specifics. It doesn't work, does it?"

"You bet your boots it works," Money said, clicking his tongue to set his pony in motion again, "Slick as slugs through a goose. Have a horse," he said, gesturing vaguely around the room. "Don't worry. They won't bite."

The young man saw that the room was crammed with rocking horses, stick horses, piles of empty beer cans. Horse masks hung from the walls. And in one corner was a huge wooden Clydesdale on wheels, from the hindquarters of which a narrow ramp extended to a small platform on which a CRT sat. The young man could see a string of constantly changing numbers flashing on the screen.

On the ramp were several hamster cages, and in each cage an undernourished rodent sprinted inside a wire wheel. The wheels were well-oiled, the young man thought, since he could hardly hear a squeak. He noticed the hamster nearest the Clydesdale's tail seemed to be tiring. In fact, the hamster abruptly stopped running altogether.

The young man took a few steps toward the Clydesdale, and he saw the lazy hamster suddenly jump in the air and commence running again. The cool green letters on the CRT said: "That's better, bucko," before they blinked out and were replaced by the string of constantly changing numbers.

Across the top of the screen, the young man could make out these words:

BRONCO BILLY'S BUDGET BUSTER
HIGH SCORE TO DATE: $2,203,354,913,666

"Please, have a horse," Money repeated.

"No thanks," the young man said, "I think I'll stand."

"Suit yourself," said Money, "but I've found a man thinks more clearly in the saddle. By the way, why are you here?"

"I'm not sure," the young man confessed.

"Excellent answer," Money smiled. "The truth is most of us aren't quite sure why we're here after meeting with the old fart."

"So you meet with him often, then?"

"Who?"

"The President."

"On the contrary," Money said, "the only time he comes to see me is when we need to reinterpret reality or restructure the facts. That's when we do the **One Minute Wishes.**"

"**One Minute Wishes?**" the young man asked. "He told me he was a **One Minute President**, but he never said anything about **One Minute Wishes.**"

"Well," Money answered, "The President tends to concentrate on the Big Picture. He sees the whole screen, if you will, and leaves it up to the rest of us to assure the set is secure and the special effects believable. **One Minute Wishes** is only the first of the three pretenses of **One Minute Presidenting.**"

"Three pretenses?"

"Surely you realize that everything happens in threes," Money said.

"No," the young man admitted, "I didn't realize that."

"Didn't it ever strike you as odd that when you subtracted the Four Horsemen of the Apocalypse from the Seven Days of the Week, you ended up with the Three Stooges?"

"No, it never crossed my mind."

"No bother that there are three one-third cups in a half-pint, three volumes in 75% of a tetralogy, three children in triplets, three lines in a tercet, or three months in a quarter?"

"Well..."

"How about three outs in an inning and three strikes to an out?"

"I've never played tennis," the young man confessed.

"Surely it must have occurred to you that Christ's arising from the grave after three days had some metaphysical meaning, or that those three guesses you got as a kid were the ghost of Dr. Jung and his collective unconscious trying to teach you something. Are you following me?"

"I don't think so," the young man confessed.

"Good," Money said. "The point, and there may not be a point, is if **One Minute Presidenting** is to be taken as the sum of its parts, it requires at least three parts from which to take its wholesomeness, and the **One Minute Wish** comprises but the first of these three essential building blocks," and Money began trotting around the room.

"Well, yes, I see, but..." the young man began.

"Of course you do, as of course you must," Money went on, bringing his trot to a gallop. "The perfect **One Minute Wish** hinges on the notion that people strive for justice. Their leaders want to be fair. People want their lives to have some meaning. Their leaders attempt to convince the world their countries mean business. People toil for security and early retirement. Presidents work for a more perfect union and a steady supply of milk chocolate. People pray for happiness. Presidents are happy. People don't want to be useless. Presidents use them. It's that simple."

Money brought his mount to a halt, reached into his pocket, pulled out a sugar cube, and popped it into his mouth. "You know," he said, "in some organizations I've worked with, the relationship between what I thought I was doing and what my boss thought I was doing were almost identical, and these were both identical with what the stockholders had chosen the boss to do. But I would end up in hot water simply for doing exactly what the stockholders voted for. Why? Because what I was doing was useless and counterproductive. What I was doing was stupid and a complete waste of time."

"But isn't it possible what you're doing here might also be stupid and a complete waste of time?" the young man asked, looking around Money's office.

"Of course it is. We all worry about that," Money said, putting his arm around the young man's shoulders. "After all, if we didn't worry about futility we wouldn't be human, would we? That's the bottom line.

"You see, some people get worried that they may be lacking in vision, but I don't. In fact, I'm quite blind," he said, waving his hand in front of his face, "but when I consider that I *am* a high-ranking government official, I realize that even if what I'm doing is completely senseless, without any value and potentially catastrophic, all I have to do is stop and make a **One Minute Wish**, which instantly reaffirms that working for the old codger surely counts for something."

"I'm sure it does," the young man marvelled, "but how does this **One Minute President** differ from all the others? How does he manage to keep his people so happy and content with all these **One Minute Wishes?**"

"Yes, it is amusing, isn't it?" Money grinned, pulling back on his hobby horse's reins and letting out a whinny. Then he trotted over to the young man, and said: "I'm going to let you in on a little secret."

"What's that?" the young man asked anxiously, his pen poised above his notepad.

"Never look a stick horse in the mouth," Money said.

The young man shook his head. He was learning so much in such a short time. And even though the information he was getting from Money about **One Minute Wishes** was a bit perplexing, he was confident the man knew exactly what he was talking about.

"I have one question," he said finally.

"Shoot," Money said.

"How do you remember all this business about **One Minute Wishes?**"

"It's easy," Money grinned. The lights dimmed, and music flooded the room, as he began to sing.

One Minute Wishes mean simply:

1.

Fairy tales can come true
It can happen to you
If you're young at heart

2.

For as rich as you are
It's much better by far
To be young at heart.

3.

And if you should survive to a hundred and five
Think of all you'll derive out of being alive.

4.

And here is the best part
You've got a head start
When you are among the very young at heart.

"You have a marvelous voice," the young man applauded.

"I know," said Money, "Everyone thinks so."

The young man made a few quick notes and began to smile. His search for an effective President was finally looking up.

"By the way," he asked, "if **One Minute Wishes** is the first pretense to becoming a **One Minute President**, what are the other two?"

"Why don't you wait and ask Mr. Ooze that?" Money asked.

The young man was amazed. "How did you know I was meeting with Mr. Ooze?"

"I wish you'd wait and ask Mr. Ooze that," Money smiled.

"Well," smiled the young man, "I guess I will. Thanks ever so much for your time."

"No sweat," Money said. "Time is something I've got plenty of these days. As you can probably tell, I'm going to be a **One Minute President** myself."

As the young man walked out the door, he took a deep, satisfying breath, held it for a few seconds, let it out, and he smiled. He didn't have the faintest idea why, but, for the first time in his life, he was really beginning to feel good.

ALL THAT SEEMED TO CHANGE abruptly when he arrived at Mr. Ooze's office. He was met by an overweight, middle-aged man who appeared to be both agitated and bored at once.

"Hello," said the young man, attempting to assert himself. "I'm..."

"Shut up and sit down," Ooze ordered.

"Yes, absolutely," agreed the young man nervously. He quickly took his place in the nearest uncomfortable chair, as Ooze seated himself and began flipping through the mounds of paper that covered his entire desktop.

While he did so, the young man glanced around the office. It was ordinary enough. Almost too ordinary. Then he noticed the walls. Or rather, noticed he could not notice the walls, for hundreds of framed certificates obscured them. Wall to wall. Floor to ceiling. Even a few on the ceiling. Certificates of every imaginable size, shape and appearance. All prominently displayed. Yet he couldn't make out what any of them were for.

"Obviously," thought the young man, "I'm in the presence of a very distinguished person."

"Well," said Ooze, looking up from his desk. "At least my Pretoria accounts are beyond scrutiny."

"I beg your pardon?"

"Later," said Ooze. "Here," and he handed the young man a sheaf of papers. "Those are over fifty sworn affidavits, mostly from people who don't exist, confirming my complete lack of knowledge on eight more Iranian arms shipments and several unreported loans."

"I'm afraid..."

"Don't be," reassured Ooze. "We can lick this thing, I'm sure of it. No need to panic."

"Mr. Ooze, I think you're making a serious mistake," explained the young man.

"That's my job, you idiot," snapped Ooze. "I've made hundreds of serious mistakes. Thousands, even. And I can continue to make them if people would just get off my back and let me get on with my duties. Weren't you briefed on this?"

"What I'm trying to tell you, is... "

"Don't try to tell me anything. Just try to tell them."

"But I don't know what you're talking about."

"Good. And neither will anyone else, if you do *your* job right."

"But you don't understand," the young man began...

"Now you're getting the picture."

"I am?"

"Of course. I'm not supposed to understand. That's the goddamn point," he sighed. "What kind of lawyer are you anyway?"

"But that's just it," said the young man. "I'm not a lawyer."

Ooze's complexion went from ruddy to ashen. "Aren't you on my staff?"

"I'm afraid not."

"Then who the hell are you?"

"I'm..."

"A reporter!" Ooze screamed. "You're a reporter!"

"Mr. Ooze..."

"No comment!"

"Mr. Ooze..."

"No comment!"

"Mr. Ooze. I'm *not* a reporter," explained the young man. "I'm just a bright, inquisitive young man in search of an effective President."

"What?"

"Really," he said. "I dropped by to ask you some questions about the **One Minute President.**"

"The **One Minute** *who*?"

"The President," said the young man.

"Well, I'm glad to hear that," said Ooze, settling into his chair. "Why don't you just relax? Stand if you want to. So you saw the old wrangler? Some hero, don't you think?"

"I suppose so," the young man responded.

"And he told you how he's a **One Minute President,** right?"

"Sure did. But it's just a lot of nonsense, isn't it?" The young man was hoping Ooze would contradict Money.

"Not at all. Half the time I'm checking the obituaries to find out if he's croaked, that's how often I see him."

"That's amazing."

"But don't get me wrong," he continued. "He's right there by my side the minute I'm about to dirty my hands with some new task or responsibility that I have absolutely no business taking on."

"You mean like **One Minute Wishes?**" pursued the young man.

"Kid's stuff," scoffed Ooze. "I'm speaking of **One Minute Gladhands.**"

"One Minute Gladhands?"

"That's right," nodded Ooze. "**One Minute Glad-hands.** They're the second pretense towards becoming a **One Minute President.**"

"You mean a simple handshake is an important step on the road to becoming an effective leader?" The young man arched his eyebrows. "It sounds rather silly, if you don't mind my saying so."

"Well I do mind your saying so," remarked Ooze. "In truth, there's nothing simple or silly about **One Minute Gladhands.** The President has managed to turn it into a profound new art form and one, I might add, that is both contagious and chain-reactive.

"**One Minute Gladhands**," Ooze continued, "are much more than your usual, effusive, insincere and offensively familiar greetings. Any elected moron can go around giving the gladhand business. But the thing is, most don't know how to use it to their advantage."

"You mean like those tests that were performed to determine one person's dominant power over another by revealing his own, distinct and highly individualized form of touch-communication?" the young man asked, taking pride in having had the good sense to renew his subscription to *Popular Psychology*.

"Of course not," Ooze said.

"Well, maybe you could give me an example of what you're talking about," the young man suggested.

"I'll go one better than that," he said, "and give you an example of an example of what I'm talking about." Ooze got up and walked around to the front of his desk.

"When I first started working here," he began, "I did absolutely nothing for a good six months. During that time, I didn't see the President at all. Not once, mind you. I kept his photograph on my desk because I was beginning to forget what he looked like.

"Then, one day, without any warning, the President just walked right into my office without knocking, and caught me sprawled on the couch, fast asleep, in just my undershirt and shorts."

"My God!" exclaimed the young man. "You must have been humiliated!"

"No, just fast asleep."

"But, I mean, he must have really torn into you, right?"

"Wrong," corrected Ooze. "What he did was wake me up—gently, I might add—hand me a cigar and congratulate me."

"What?"

"As a matter of fact," continued Ooze, "he kept shaking my hand, slapping my back and smiling from ear to ear as he told me how proud he was to have me on his team."

"But..."

"Then he said something," Ooze recounted, "that actually helped make my job simpler, easier and more comfortable than ever before."

"And what was that?" the young man asked, notebook open and pencil poised.

"He simply said, 'Let's do it,'" Ooze remembered fondly.

"That's it?"

"That was plenty, believe me. The next day, I received a ridiculously fat raise, my own private jet and a box of candy." Ooze stuck his chest out so far that a button on his jacket popped off, narrowly missing the young man's eye. "I can proudly say," he said proudly, "that the whole episode changed my life dramatically."

The young man shook his head, visibly frustrated. "Let me get this straight," he said. "The President catches you asleep at your post, and he ends up showering you with gifts. I don't get it."

"You're not a very fast learner, are you?" questioned Ooze. "All you have to remember is that it's not whether you do something right or wrong that matters, but the fact that you are doing whatever it is you happen to be doing at any given time when these **One Minute Gladhands** occur.

"We have a very popular motto around here that serves to remind us of our own participation in **One Minute Gladhands**," Ooze said. "It goes like this:

Never Mind

What People Are Doing

Simply Tell Them

To Keep On Doing It

"And don't forget," Ooze continued, "**One Minute Gladhands,** when properly administered, have a giddy effect on people. Once the momentum is underway, the chain reaction is virtually unstoppable."

"So," offered the young man, "a person's job-performance, or -nonperformance, has no bearing on the administration or receipt of the **One Minute Gladhands.**"

"Precisely," said Ooze.

"But don't you think people want the truth?"

"If they did," Ooze countered, "they wouldn't eat out."

The young man made note of this in his book.

"The thing to keep in mind," Ooze said, as he walked back behind his desk and sat down, "is that the **One Minute President** never responds to who or what or where I am. That would be a complete waste of time. After all, it only takes a minute to set someone up."

"And that's why it's called a One Minute Gladhand," said the young man, visibly proud that he was able to figure that one out all by himself. He proceeded to jot down all that he was learning. After careful deliberation, he concluded that:

The **One Minute Gladhand** works best when you:

1.
Do what you think.

2.
Think what you feel.

3.
Feel what you want.

4
Want what you like.

5.
Like what you do, to do what you do.

6.
Do woppa do woppa do.

7.
And tell a friend.

"So what's the third pretense?" the young man asked apprehensively.

"You can find that out for yourself, when you meet with Mrs. Bierfurter. You are scheduled to meet with her, aren't you?"

"Yes," admitted the young man. "But how did you know?"

"It's my hobby," answered Ooze.

"Yes, well I guess that explains that," said the young man. And he turned toward the door.

"By the way," he remarked, turning back around, "I couldn't help but notice all these certificates you have framed on the walls."

"Yes, aren't they something?" Ooze beamed. "I'm going to get a bigger office once I run out of ceiling-space."

"You must have worked incredibly hard and impressed quite a few people to receive so many."

"I gave them to myself. It's a slight variation on the **One Minute Gladhand** I dreamed up on my own," he said proudly. "It's starting to catch on, too. A clerk over in General Accounting already has an impressive collection of shrunken heads."

The young man had to smile. Ooze was obviously very sharp, he thought. "Well," he finally said, "I've taken up too much of your time already. Thanks for your help."

"Anytime," offered Ooze. "Time, besides money, is one thing I know how to spend well. Come see me again if you want a job. But you'd better hurry. Once I get to be a **One Minute Supreme Court Justice**, I won't be bought cheap.

"Confidentially," whispered Ooze, "it's my **One Minute Wish**."

The young man wanted to think about all he was absorbing, so he left the building and took a walk around the grounds. He thought about what he had been told so far about the **One Minute President's** system of government. "How can you argue with people who are so thoroughly committed to all this?" he thought. "But do **One Minute Gladhands** really work?" he asked himself. "Does all this **One Minute** mumbo-jumbo really produce an effective government?" He decided to return to the **One Minute President's** secretary and ask her to reschedule his appointment with Mrs. Bierfurter.

NICE TO SEE YOU AGAIN SO SOON," the secretary said when she saw him walk in.

"Thank you, but I was hoping you could reschedule my appointment..."

"I've already taken care of that," she interrupted. "Mrs. Bierfurter said to tell you that any time tomorrow morning is fine with her."

"But how..."

"I'm perfectly capable of doing my job, young man."

"Well, then perhaps you could..."

"Make that appointment you were about to ask me to make? It's all been arranged. Here's the address," and she handed him a slip of paper which he numbly reached for. "You're to see Ms. Fester, chief curator at the Museum of National Antiquity. She'll expect you at 2 P.M., sharp."

The young man gave out a barely audible "thank you" and then slipped away very quietly.

SHORTLY BEFORE 2 P.M., the young man arrived at the Museum of National Antiquity, an eight-story structure of pink granite and glass that occupied an entire city block. He was only slightly surprised to find the building empty and deserted. By now the young man had come to understand how closely the absence of clutter was tied to efficiency in the **One Minute Way of Life.**

The young man walked across the lobby to where a large sign said:

TO ASSURE PROMPT SERVICE
PLEASE TAKE A NUMBER
AND HAVE A SEAT

On the wall under the sign was a display that said:

NOW SERVING
66

And sure enough when the young man checked, the number he had taken from the dispenser was 67. It pleased him that he wouldn't have long to wait. In fact, even before he had managed to locate a chair on the ground floor, he heard footsteps behind him and a voice called out: "Number 67?"

The young man turned to acknowledge the voice and was struck by the awesome beauty of a statuesque woman in a gossamer white gown who seemed to float over the marble toward him. He managed to say: "I'm number 67. I have an appointment with Ms. Fester."

"Call me Helen," Ms. Fester smiled.

"Helen," the young man said.

"That's better. Now follow me," she instructed, as she wafted by him. She led him down a wide hallway and up three flights of stairs to a set of ten-foot high polished walnut doors. In large gilt letters on the door were these words:

THE HALL OF FAILED POLICIES OF THE PAST

"Give me a hand," Helen said, and together they leaned against one of the large wooden doors until it slowly swung inward, revealing a cavernous auditorium piled from floor to ceiling with books and artwork.

"I don't understand," said the young man, "The rest of the building is spotless and spacious. Why is everything crammed in this room?"

"Budget reductions," Helen said. "I was forced to lay off the entire work force."

"I don't see what that has to do with the emptiness of the rest of the place and the chaos in here."

"It's really quite simple," Helen explained. "When I came here from the Bureau of the Ulterior, we had a staff of nearly 500 people and one of the largest collections of artwork and objects of historical significance ever assembled anywhere on the planet. The net cost of this operation was in the neighborhood of $5 per year for every man woman and child in this country."

"I see," said the young man.

"But the actual cost was much higher. Janitorial service, for instance, was contracted out. So was security, procurement, and so on. And what good were all these expenditures doing? Were they strengthening the national defense? Were they contributing to the education and enlightenment of the general population?"

"Well," the young man hemmed, "that would at least seem to be the purpose of a museum."

"I'm surprised that a young man as bright and inquisitive as you appear to be would think such rubbish. Surely you realize that most museums are only open during hours the general population is at work. It's obvious the only reason museums exist is to give wealthy members of our society huge living rooms in which to display some of their favorite momentos."

"I'd never thought of it that way," he said, jotting down this new thought in his book.

"So what I undertook to do when I came here was let this particular museum be self-supporting, since budget constraints make it impossible to pay for any salary beyond my own. I decided to allow the collection to sink or swim on the free market. The result of those efforts is what you see today."

"You sold the collection?"

"Auctioned leases to the collection," Helen Fester stressed. "The things you see in this room are the objects no one was willing to lease, not even at a dollar an acre. I've stored them here in the event some future administration can find an interested party to lease them at a later date."

The young man was impressed. "That was a stroke of genius."

"Yes," said Helen Fester, "I thought so myself."

A short, uneasy silence followed.

Then quite without warning, the young man was surprised to hear himself ask this question: "Do you have any idea why I'm here?"

"Not the slightest," Helen smiled, "unless you were expecting me to say that the **One Minute President's** government is not the most efficient on Earth."

"That's exactly why I'm here," he said.

"Then I'm sorry to disappoint you," she said, "because there has never, in all the history of mankind, been a more efficient government than the **One Minute President's.**"

"But how can that be?" the young man asked. "How can a country built upon wishes and gladhands have the most efficient government in the world?"

"Beats me."

Just then an alarm blared and a voice boomed in the Hall of Failed Policies of the Past. "Your minute is up," the voice said. "Get out!"

The young man departed the Museum of National Antiquity shaking his head. The **One Minute President** was a complete enigma to him.

That night the young man could hardly sleep. Twice he found himself dreaming he was on stage dressed like Elvis Presley playing the part of Hamlet with his mouth full of knockwurst, while a leather-clad Ophelia stomped Polonius to death with her high heels. The young man took this to be an omen, a message that he did not have all the pieces to the puzzle yet. And each time he awoke in a sweat, he found himself truly excited about the next day—when he would learn the final pretense to becoming a **One Minute President.**

WHEN THE YOUNG MAN arrived at Mrs. Bierfurter's office the next morning, he was greeted by an attractive woman in her late 90's, clad in bib overalls, who led him into a large greenhouse. "Pull up a cactus and make yourself comfortable," she urged.

"This certainly is an impressive greenhouse, Mrs. Bierfurter," said the young man, glancing around.

"Of course it is," she huffed. "Beyond the bromeliads, I've got five species of orchid here that no longer exist in the wild."

"That's very nice," said the young man, "But I'm here because..."

"Oh, I know why you're here, all right," said Mrs. Bierfurter, checking for aphids on the underside of the leaves of a tall rubber plant. "You've been to see the rummy, and you think he's just the neatest guy you'd ever want to meet."

"Well, yes," the young man admitted, "Yes, he is," no longer uneasy about expressing his complete and abject adoration of the old galoot.

"And he told you all about being a **One Minute President**, didn't he?"

"Well, yes," the young man said, "but it's all a bunch of falderal, isn't it?" He was still hoping he'd find someone with a bad word to say about the **One Minute Method**.

"That depends on what *falderal* means," Mrs. Bierfurter answered. "But the truth is I hardly ever see the old coot."

"You mean you don't have much contact with him outside your regular weekly meetings?"

"I never see him at all, except on the TV."

"But don't you need to see him on a regular basis?"

"Whatever would I need to see him for?" Mrs. Bierfurter asked, quite seriously. "If the geezer needs to talk to me, he can give me a call. We do, of course, occasionally attend the same diplomatic or social functions, and I do provide the floral arrangements when he entertains, but for the most part, I prefer to watch his occasional news conference and the late night movies."

"But this seems to fly in the face of **One Minute Wishes** and **One Minute Gladhands**," the young man argued.

"I suppose it does," Mrs. Bierfurter mused, "but then there are *three* pretenses to **One Minute Presidenting**."

"Of course," said the young man. "And that's why I'm here, to learn the final pretense."

"And you'll learn it soon enough," said the woman, swatting at two flies copulating on the potting bench. "And you'll see why I think the wishes and gladhands are hen scrabble."

"So what exactly do you do in the administration?" the young man asked, taking notes and following the woman as she bustled among her plants, feeding, pruning, and hand-picking pests.

"Oh, I'm not with the administration. My son is Secretary of Ultimate Solutions."

The young man was stunned. "But..." he fumbled. "But what do you do?"

"That's obvious, isn't it?" Mrs. Bierfurter asked. "I putter around the greenhouse and answer the phone when it rings."

And, as if on cue, the phone rang. Mrs. Bierfurter shuffled past the young man to the far end of the greenhouse, shouting: "I'm coming. I'm coming.

"Who is it and what do you want?" the old woman barked into the mouthpiece. "Of course this is Mrs. Bierfurter, who else would it be? What?... So they did, did they?" and she picked a hornworm off a nearby tomato plant, popped it into her mouth, and cracked it like chewing gum. "Well, go ahead and put some more plutonium in the reservoirs, for starters... That'll keep them busy for awhile. I said that'll keep them busy for awhile. And then," she said, spitting the hornworm's husk at a cluster of harlequin beetles, "put the Pacific fleet on full alert and have the Marines invade Puerto Rico to collect delinquent parking fines." She listened for a second, then smiled and said: "Well, you're welcome, you old goat. That's what I'm here for. Yes. I love you too." Then she hung up and shuffled back to the young man.

"I couldn't help overhearing," he said. "Do you mind my asking what that was all about?"

"Oh, nothing really," Mrs. Bierfurter said, pinching a sucker off a Better Boy. "One of the papers ran an editorial calling for the resignation of Mr. Ooze."

"But you just..."

"Now listen," she snapped, "You came here to learn the final pretense to **One Minute Presidenting**, didn't you?"

"Well, yes, I did," the young man said, "but ..."

"Well," she chortled, "you were just within earshot of the final pretense: the **One Minute Retaliation**."

"The **One Minute Retaliation**?"

"So you heard me the first time," Mrs. Bierfurter said, "Come along now."

As the young man followed the old woman to a soiled bench where she undertook the task of repotting a bonzai Monterey Pine, he tried very hard to take notes without appearing too confused.

"Have you any idea," Mrs. Bierfurter continued, as she hoisted a 50-pound bag of pig manure onto the potting bench, "what the difference is between how our government is run today and how it was run twenty years ago?"

"Well, I..."

"Your time's up. But I'll tell you what the difference is. The difference is our government is totally committed to obliterating the myth of intelligence."

"It is?" the young man asked.

"Don't you think so?" she smiled, pinching his cheek, "I'd say we're doing one helluva job."

"Thank you," the young man blushed, "But what does this have to do with **One Minute Retaliations?**"

"Nothing," said Mrs. Bierfurter, squashing a slug with her thumb, "except that it helps create fear, and fear itself is the greatest communicator. Without fear, Franklin Delano Roosevelt would have been just another polio victim. After all, you can gladhand people all you want and listen to their wishes, but when it comes to the bottom line, the only thing that really keeps people straight is abject terror. And that's where the **One Minute Retaliation** comes in."

"You know," the young man nodded, "I think I'm beginning to understand what you're talking about."

"I'd like to believe you," Mrs. Bierfurter smiled, "But my geraniums know better."

"They do?"

"Why not ask them?" she said, picking up her scythe and hacking away at a row of hanging fuchsias. "Suppose I were to ask you what makes this the most powerful country on the face of the earth," she proposed. "What would your answer be?"

"We are a free people, united in the belief in the hopes and ideals of representative democracy," the young man said quickly, "defenders of the rights of all men, regardless of race, religion, or immune system deficiency."

The old woman shook her head in frustration. "This isn't a Civics test, stripling," she said, "Even Flipper is more perceptive than that."

"Michael Jackson?" he offered, "Stars Wars? The Los Angeles Raiders? No, wait, it's on the tip of my tongue..."

"Sure it is, but never mind that," Mrs. Bierfurter said in disgust, flinging her scythe at a dwarf banana tree. "The fact is, this is the most powerful nation on earth because it possesses more ways to eradicate all the life on this planet than all the other nations combined."

"I had no idea you wanted the facts," the young man pouted, "Up until now nothing about the **One Minute Method** had anything to do with the facts."

"And with good reason," Mrs. Bierfurter said.

"But up until now," the young man said, "Nothing I'd learned about the **One Minute Method** had anything to do with reason."

"And there was a purpose to that," smiled the old woman.

"But up until now," the young man frowned, "Nothing I'd learned about the **One Minute Method** led me to believe there was any purpose behind it."

"Which is just as well," Mrs. Bierfurter said.

The young man bore down, licking the tip of his pencil. "So what exactly are you getting at?"

"Simply this," said Mrs. Bierfurter, as she picked up a hoe for emphasis. "The most powerful nation on earth can only be the most powerful nation on earth not because it possesses superior weaponry, but because it possesses the notion and determination to use it, whenever it feels like it."

"Yes," said the young man. "I've studied the concept of nuclear deterrence."

"Screw nuclear deterrence!" Mrs. Bierfurter shouted, swinging the hoe within a centimeter of the young man's head. "Can't you get it through that inquisitive young skull of yours?" She held the hoe like an M-16, pointing it at the young man's abdomen. "We've got the power to do whatever we damn well please, and that's what makes the **One Minute Retaliation** such a useful, non-negotiable tool when dealing with both local and global vandalism."

"But it sounds like you're suggesting ... "

"Suggesting?" the old woman shrieked. "I am not suggesting anything! I'm telling you: the use of force, with extreme prejudice, should always be the first solution to any problem, and don't you ever forget it!" And with that, Mrs. Bierfurter brought the hoe down hard on one of her rare orchids, splitting the flower in two. "Never could stand the beauty of that species," she frowned, "African."

The young man decided to look busy by scribbling in his book and, in doing so, made the discovery that his penmanship was improving. He couldn't read a thing he had written. This pleased him a great deal, since, although his notes had never made any sense, now he couldn't read them at all.

"Let me also emphasize," Mrs. Bierfurter continued, tossing the mangled orchid on her compost heap, "that when I speak of problems, I'm not just talking about problems overseas. I'm talking about problems right here at home."

"You mean the unions?"

"The unemployment offices," she corrected him. "This country is swarming with obsolete people determined to say they are still out of work, though the statistics we struggle to invent prove they are no longer eligible for benefits."

"You think we should nuke the unemployed?" asked the young man.

"It's certainly an option," she argued. "But why bother with the expense when TV is so much cheaper and twice as effective?"

"I don't understand."

"Tell me something I don't already know," Mrs. Bierfurter smiled. "But either way you look at it: once those missiles hit their targets, the recipients of a **One Minute Retaliation** are almost always taken by surprise."

"I imagine it must make people think twice..."

"You haven't listened to a thing I've said, have you?" she asked. The young man started to answer, but Mrs. Bierfurter began to laugh.

"That's terrific," the young man said, helping Mrs. Bierfurter out of the compost heap. "How did you learn to do that?"

"Simply," Mrs. Bierfurter answered, "by watching the old lummox do it himself."

"You mean the President can laugh until he needs CPR?" the astonished young man asked.

"Well, not all the time," Mrs. Bierfurter admitted. "Usually he just chuckles, like the rest of us. But now and then he likes to split a gut. And when he does, it has a positive effect on everyone around him."

"He must be pretty stable," the young man suggested.

"Steady as a tombstone," Mrs. Bierfurter answered.

The young man was impressed. He was beginning to see how valuable such a President was to a country that had had so little to laugh at in the past two decades.

"So why do you think **One Minute Retaliations** are so effective?" he asked.

"I think you better ask Methuselah yourself," Mrs. Bierfurter said, as she picked up a chain saw and walked the young man to the door. "I've got to get back to my little rascals."

When he thanked her for her time, she winked and said: "Time is something I wish I had a bit more of." And they both howled. He was beginning to feel like a member of the family rather than a solicitor, and that made him feel just fine.

As soon as he was out in the hall, he realized how much time he had spent with Mrs. Bierfurter and how little information she had given him. He reflected on what she had said, consulted his notes, and began to hear a pleasant tune pop into his head, as he formulated in his own mind what you should do whenever you feel like it:

The **One Minute Retaliation** works best:

1. When you wish upon a star
   Makes no difference who you are
   When you wish upon a star
   Your dreams come true

THE FIRST HALF OF THE RETALIATION

2. Act immediately and ruthlessly.
3. Give people fifteen minutes to evacuate the target.
4. Tell people how fortunate they are that you don't destroy the entire planet.
5. Stop for a few seconds of terrifying silence to let everyone realize how thoroughly pissed you are.

THE SECOND HALF OF THE RETALIATION

6. Offer emergency aid to the devastated areas.
7. Speak kindly of the dead.
8. Reaffirm your right and responsibility to modify behavior by any means at hand.
9. Realize that although you were not able to escalate this retaliation into a full scale conventional war, there will be other opportunities.

The young man was not at all surprised to find himself heading toward the office of the **One Minute President,** marveling at the simplicity of the **One Minute Method.**

All three of the pretenses—**Wishes, Gladhands,** and **Retaliations**—made absolutely no sense, and as such they bore up well against all logic and any rational observation. "But why do they work?" he still wondered. "Why is the **One Minute President** considered the most efficient and nicest guy on the face of the Earth?"

WHEN THE YOUNG MAN ENTERED the President's office, he was once again greeted enthusiastically by the **One Minute President**, who urged him to be seated in the sofa-chair while he positioned himself behind the podium.

"So tell me," the President coaxed, "what did you learn about my system of government?"

"More than I bargained for," admitted the young man. "I found out that there are three pretenses towards becoming a **One Minute President: Wishes, Gladhands** and **Retaliations.**"

"And how does all this strike you?"

"Well," the young man admitted, "I can honestly say your system of government is definitely the most effective operation I've ever experienced. But," and the young man scratched his head, "I still don't understand why it works."

"That's perfectly understandable," he said, "considering that you don't work for me."

"But the people who do work for you don't seem to understand why it works," the young man countered.

The President smiled. "All you have to understand is that you don't have to understand why it works to understand why it works."

The young man was quick to make note of this in his book.

"With that in mind," continued the President. "I stand here eagerly reluctant to withhold any and all information to help you grasp a working knowledge of what it is I'm supposed to tell you. Where would you like to start?"

"Well, to begin with, when you talk about **One Minute Presidenting**, are you really saying that it only takes a minute to do all the things you need to do as a **One Minute President?**"

"To be perfectly honest, no," he confessed. "Most of the time it only takes about 60 seconds. But if I went around calling myself a 60-Second President, I might get sued by a television network for trade-mark infringement, and I don't think too many people would believe me if I got sued. So I chose a more symbolic term, which enabled me to round out the title, as well as the time sequence."

"You mean it actually takes *less* than a minute to accomplish everything you hope to accomplish?"

"Not really," said the President. "But that's unimportant. You see, getting your own way and getting people to do what you want can be easily incorporated into a very tight and manipulative quick-fix procedure. It really doesn't take as long as you might think.

"Let me show you one of my favorite platitudes," he offered, fingering the familiar remote-control device that he removed from his pocket. "It's a saying well worth repeating several times a day. Watch the screen."

The Best Minute I Spend Is When

The Rates Are Cheaper

Past 11 PM

"Now," began the President. "Let me put this in perspective. What I've been able to do in this administration is take the essentials of any program and foster the infrastructure of democratic idealism to a point beyond any real and meaningful relationship between a government and its people. In a single, bold stroke my system has achieved a realignment that has produced countless ways to ensure the risk of economic collapse, social unrest and nuclear catastrophe —both by accident and design."

"But that sounds frightening."

"Doesn't it, though?" mused the President. "And yet, when you really look at how things are, rather than how things might be, you begin to wish that the dawning of an innovative new age is not only possible but probable. All because of our ability to muster the strength to continue the course that charts itself on a crusade for national upheaval.

"Just think," beamed the President. "We are the greatest and most powerful nation ever. And it takes a very special and most peculiar brand of common sense to realize the unobtainable, ignore the obvious and perceive whatever future remains—ever-mindful that the world will go on sliding toward disaster no matter what we do."

"That's really interesting," the young man confessed. "But I still don't understand what you're talking about."

"Good, good," reassured the President. "Ignorance and stupidity are admirable traits in our youth of today. Especially among those who are willing to delude themselves into accepting the proven misjudgments of others."

"That's very kind," the young man said, "but perhaps I could get to the bottom of all this if I could put some of my *why* questions to you."

"Certainly," smiled the President. "After *who* questions and *where* questions, *why* questions are my favorite."

"Great. Then let me start with **One Minute Wishes.** Why do they work so well?"

P ROBABLY THE BEST WAY TO explain to you why **One Minute Wishes** work," said the President, "would be to tell you a story. Stories always seem to have a way of arousing enthusiasm in a great many people who, for the most part, have given up searching for new and normal avenues of comprehension.

"When I was a much, much younger man than I am today," he began, "I took a job with a small, Midwestern radio station in a small, Midwestern town, populated by small, Midwestern people. I was hired to do play-by-play announcing for this particular town's bush-league baseball team, broadcasting all their home games to surrounding areas that still bothered to receive the station's weak, low-watt signal.

"Anyway," explained the President. "Since the station didn't have the means or the ambition to provide on-the-spot coverage, I would remain in the studio behind my microphone while another employee was at the ballpark relaying the events of the game back to me, using Morse Code. I would then transcribe all the little dots and dashes into a more familiar language —usually English—and, with the help of one of those sound-effect recordings that duplicated the actual noise of hotdog-eating, beer-swilling, hometown-cussing fans, I'd 'broadcast' the entire game from the safe confines of a recording booth."

At this point, the young man barely succeeded in stifling a yawn.

"Well," the President continued. "One afternoon, as the game was going into the bottom of the ninth with the home team coming to bat and trailing by three runs, the telegraph line went dead! For a split second, I panicked and started to read an old 'Amos 'n Andy' script, playing both parts, hoping the telegraph would come back up. But it didn't. So what do you suppose I did next?"

"Switched to a commercial announcement?" guessed the young man.

"I made up the rest of the game," the President chuckled. "I had the first three batters get consecutive base hits to load the bases. Then I had the next batter hit a grand slam to win the game for the home team," and he laughed at his own ingenuity. "I can honestly say it was the most thrilling climax to a baseball game that anyone in that small, Midwestern town had ever heard."

"But how did the game turn out?"

"I don't recall. But in the end, it really didn't matter."

"But why not?"

"Because with the thousands of people who heard the game," explained the President, "versus the handful of people who actually saw the game, the overwhelming majority believed the home team had indeed won.

"There they were: on the edges of their seats, chewing their knuckles, the volume on their radios up full blast, wishing it would come true and then hearing it with their own ears. The truth is, it simply was too good to be true, disproving the theorem that 'seeing is believing,' and replacing it with 'wishing is believing.'"

"But it was a lie," the young man protested.

"It was a wish that came true," corrected the President.

"But it didn't really happen," he persisted.

"But it did happen, don't you see?" said the President. "Their yearnings, hankerings, hopes and aspirations were fulfilled because they had wished it to happen. That was all that really mattered. I was merely the instrument that helped guide their wish to delusion."

"So in other words," pondered the young man out loud, "if people can be led to believe their wishes can come true—even when they don't come true—then what they wish for and what they don't get are really one and the same thing. And since what they're really wishing for—apart from the actual intent of the wish itself—is what they're really getting, the consequence of the entire wishing process becomes a subsequent result of their own wishful thinking—in a perverse sort of way."

"Exactly!" exclaimed the **One Minute President**. "And I couldn't have said it better myself."

The young man was delighted with his host's affirmation, and equally delighted with his own progress towards reaching a better appreciation of the principles of **One Minute Presidenting**.

"As you've no doubt gathered thus far," said the President, "all this is directly linked, once again, to how you interpret the notion of readjusting reality.

"I remember reading a wonderful story about Senator Joe McCarthy a few years ago. At the height of his popularity, someone asked him how he could claim to know for certain that a number of communists were dating the sons and daughters of men who were members of the Knights of Columbus. It was reported that McCarthy answered by simply smiling and tapping his head."

"You're joking."

"No, I'm not joking. He later claimed he never cluttered his mind with proof that could be substantiated by anyone but himself. Just think of that," the President said. "He had the right idea, but the wrong notion."

The young man nodded and decided not to ask if Senator Joe McCarthy was the same guy who sang with the Beatles.

The President then produced the remote-control again.

"This brings to mind another important saying that I think you're ready to appreciate at this point in our discussion," he said. "It's always served to remind me of the simplicity inherent in our human nature," and the President clicked the gadget.

When You're In A Hurry

And You're Not Really Sure

If It's Easy And Convenient

It's The Law

The young man was busy writing this in his notebook when the President shut the screen down and said, "Now I'll let you in on another little secret that's absolutely vital to the success of **One Minute Wishes**—Statistics."

"Statistics?"

"Statistics," stressed the President. "The ability to rattle off statistics to buttress a **One Minute Wish**, whether it's in the course of a face-to-face encounter with a single person or an image-to-image confrontation with an entire nation, is a necessary ingredient in relating the notion of that wish.

"If I'm foolish enough to walk into a press conference, or go before the cameras without taking advantage of a vast amount of imaginative statistical data
which has little to do with the answers I give, then I
don't deserve to call myself a **One Minute President**."

"Could you give me an example of how it works?"
asked the young man.

"I'll give you several examples," he volunteered.
"Take unemployment. Some critics say that since I
took office, more people have lost their jobs than at
any time in history. But statistics show the jobless rate
has actually dropped 58% while the job force increased
nearly 62%, and there are now 4.7 more jobs for people
to choose from, on a ratio of 6 to 1, than the previous
3.8 on an adjustable curve of 29% over the maximum
index allowed under a minimum 14% spending
limit."

"That's astounding," said the young man. "But
what's it mean?"

"It means that statistics are more useful, more per-
suasive and more impressive than facts," explained
the President. "And they're fun, besides.

"Take the military budget," he continued. "What we
spend on national defense today is actually $250 billion
less than what was spent before a 4% tax levied against
coffee imports, dating back to 1792. The entire MX
missile program costs less than a year's free school
lunches for the children in Maui. That doesn't even
take into account the annual birthrate of 1.4 babies
born to every man, woman, and child living on 72% of
the nation's federally-subsidized farmlands."

The young man worked hard and fast to write all
these figures down, not wanting to miss a single
decimal point and hoping the President would be
impressed by his attention to detail.

"Did you know," the President went on, "that the 20% capital gains rate allows your average wage-earner, making a mere $200,000 annually, to realize a total tax savings of a measly 83% on any investment under the current depreciation schedule of .0015%?"

"That's news to me," confessed the young man.

"And did you realize that more than 91% of those receiving welfare payments have at one time or another held 8-1/2% passbook accounts with an annual yield of 9%—requiring a minimum deposit of $1,000?"

"I had no idea," the young man admitted.

"Or did you further know," queried the President, "that it would take more than 1,200 coal miners working 16 hours a day, 7 days a week for 22 years, to make as much money as Frank Sinatra makes in a week, but they would never sing so sweetly?"

"Now that one I did know," the young man beamed, visibly proud that he wasn't appearing to be totally ignorant.

"So there you have it," said the **One Minute President**. "A concise formula for **One Minute Wishes** that can't fail if you have the determination and imagination to make things up as you go along."

"I'm impressed by the sheer tomfoolery of it," remarked the young man. "And it works, too."

"Of course you are, and of course it does," smiled the President.

The **One Minute President** then removed his wristwatch and said, "Perhaps you noticed that everyone who works for me wears one of these," and he tossed the watch to the young man. "Press the upper-left button once," he instructed, "and watch the LCD."

Take A Minute To:

Cross Your Fingers
Close Your Eyes
Plug Your Ears
With Pumpkin Pies

Crack Your Toes
Lick Your Lips
Pick Your Nose
And Make A Wish

"That's very inspirational," the young man remarked, making a quick note of this in his book, and then returned the President's watch.

"So, what's next?" asked the **One Minute President.**

"Well, perhaps, if it's all right with you, we could move on to **One Minute Gladhands.**"

"You bet," said the **One Minute President.** "And knowing you, I suppose you'll be wanting to know why they work, too, right?"

"It would certainly help."

A CTUALLY," SAID THE **ONE** Minute President, "**One Minute Gladhands** are probably the easiest to explain of the three pretenses. And the easiest to understand, too. In fact, I'm a bit surprised that you don't know why they work."

"I guess it's because I haven't had the opportunity to experience many **One Minute Gladhands**," justified the young man, embarrassed by his own specific gravity.

The President laughed. "Are you serious?"

"What do you mean?"

"Young man, ever since we first met you've been the unfaltering recipient of numerous **One Minute Gladhands.**"

"I have?"

"Of course you have. I'd even go so far as to say that both our meetings could be construed as two lengthy extensions of the basic principle embodied in a **One Minute Gladhand.**"

"You mean the manner in which you shook my hand each time I arrived and the last time I left?" asked the young man, trying hard not to sound ridiculous.

"Don't be ridiculous," chastised the President. "Those handshakes are just a minor formality. I'm talking about the POF Principle."

"The POF Principle?" echoed the young man. "What's that?"

"The Pretense of Friendliness," said the President. "And any **One Minute Gladhand** worth delivering isn't worth a damn unless it's backed by the POF Principle. Here let me show you what I mean." And together they walked over to the President's favorite blank wall.

"Now pay careful attention," the President said, "It's not every day you gain wisdom." And the young man watched as the President stood motionless, staring at the wall in complete silence.

After ten minutes of this, the young man felt the muscles in his back and neck beginning to grow numb, and he began to worry about the President, whose eyes, he had noticed, had begun to roll skyward, leaving only the whites exposed.

"Mr. President?" he said softly.

The President continued to stare at the wall.

"Mr. President?" he said loudly.

"Mr. President?" he finally shouted.

But still the President gave no indication that he had heard him.

Panic stricken, the young man gripped the President's shoulders and shook him. "Mr. President?" he cried. "Are you all right?"

"So there you are!" the President said suddenly as he turned and smiled at the startled young man. "For a minute there I thought I'd lost you." Then he shook the young man's hand and said, "Glad to have you back."

"Glad to have *me* back?" the young man started to protest.

"That's right!" chuckled the **One Minute President**. "*Glad* to have you back."

And it suddenly dawned on the young man what had just occurred. "Yes, I get it," the young man chortled, "Glad to have you back."

And together, the two men so much enjoyed the laugh they shared that before long they were both doubled up and rolling on the floor.

But when the young man remembered what Mrs. Bierfurter had told him about the President and CPR, he decided to stop laughing, and he helped the hysterical President to his feet, walking him to the podium and standing beside him until he was certain there'd been no cardiac arrest.

The young man sat back down in the sofa-chair and almost began laughing again as he watched the President desperately try to catch his breath. "He's quite a guy," thought the young man. "Quite a guy."

Finally, after several feeble attempts to breathe normally, the President regained his composure and wiped his eyes. "Well," he smiled, "I guess we both needed that."

"We certainly did," agreed the young man.

"The last time I enjoyed a good laugh like that was the night they woke me to say I'd been reelected," and the President guffawed thoughtfully.

The young man made a few notes and then put his notebook down. He thought about everything that had just happened. He was now beginning to see **One Minute Presidenting** for what it was—an immensely impractical, highly successful, political reconstitution of the shaggy dog story.

He was dazzled by how well something as simple and shallow as the **One Minute Gladhand** worked. What's more, he was his own best example. It was a very clever pretense—if not the cleverest.

"You know," said the young man, "I think I'm beginning to appreciate why the people who work for you enjoy it so much when they receive a **One Minute Gladhand**."

"Well, if you can understand that," said the **One Minute President**, "then you can probably understand why **Gladhands** are so effective when administered to an entire nation—the **National One Minute Gladhand**, if you will. Never before in the history of this great nation has a single **Gladhand** been able to persuade so many people at any one time to carry on with whatever they're doing, secure in their own insensibility that what's behind their TV screen is more than just tiny tubes and transistors. When 250 million people turn on their TV sets, and I'm on—I'm really on."

"It makes you want to visualize the future," the young man chimed in.

"Young man, I can relate to you with the utmost assurance," and he paused a moment to visualize the future, "that the day is not far off when people will be fortunate enough to stay at home, turn on their sets, sit back, relax, and vote for the candidate of their predetermined choice—all without ever having to put their shoes on to kick the dog."

"Something like that would boost a network's ratings," commented the young man without looking up, still feverishly scribbling in his notebook.

"And if by chance," the President added, "they don't quite get the picture the first time around, we simply go back to **One Minute Wishes** again until they do."

"And after **Wishes** again," the young man asked, "do you do **Gladhands** again?"

"Absolutely," he agreed. Then, looking the young man right in the eyes, the President walked up to him, shook his hand firmly and said, "You're an easygoing, outgoing, ongoing young man, with a fair idea of what's going on. That makes me feel very comfortable in my uneasiness to be sharing the secrets of **One Minute Presidenting** with you." And they smiled at one another, for they both knew a **One Minute Gladhand** when they heard one.

"I think I understand now why **One Minute Wishes** and **One Minute Gladhands** work," said the young man, "even if I don't understand why I understand they work."

"That's the spirit."

"But I don't think I understand why I don't understand why **One Minute Retaliations** work," he said.

"I can understand that," the President sympathized. "But I hope you'll feel the same way after I get through explaining them to you."

THERE ARE SEVERAL REASONS why the **One Minute Retaliation** works so well," the President said. "To begin with, everybody's read Norman Mailer, and you know what he said."

The young man nodded and smiled, hoping the President didn't really expect him to recite what Norman Mailer said, especially since he had no idea who he was.

"I was born; I suffer; I am guilty," the President went on, "that's what Mailer said."

The young man wrinkled his eyebrows, not because he doubted what the President was saying but rather because his mother had taught him it was impolite to ask where the restroom was, especially at the Presidential level.

"Or if it wasn't Mailer," the President added, eyeing the young man closely, "it was someone else. Do you see what I'm driving at?"

"Of course," said the young man, closing his eyes, "you're onto an eagle on the fourth hole in Augusta during the Masters. You're twelve under par, playing in a foursome with Larry, Moe, and Curly."

"You're a fast learner," the President said.

"I've had a good teacher," the young man smiled, "but I still don't see what this has to do with **One Minute Retaliations.**"

"I was getting to that," the President said as he stepped from behind the podium and approached the young man, holding a fan of Tally-Ho's in his left hand, "Pick a card, any card."

Mildly amused, the young man picked the Jack of Spades as the President said, "Now don't tell me what card you've picked. Just put it in the stack and shuffle the cards carefully."

The young man did as he was told, giving the deck back to the President when he was through.

"Do you remember what your card was?" the President asked, winking at the young man, who nodded and watched the President's hands as he cut the cards several times and finally held the Deuce of Clubs up, saying: "Because this is your card."

The young man laughed and said: "Sorry, sir, but I picked the Jack of Spades."

The President smiled, reached inside his suit jacket and produced a .44 magnum revolver which he pointed at the young man's head.

"Now wait a second," the young man stammered, "What's all this about?"

"You picked the wrong card," the President explained, "but let me stress I have nothing against you personally, and I still value the fact that you are an inquisitive and ambitious young man who knows what's going on. Let's try it again, shall we?"

"But I...,"

"Then don't pick another card." the President said, cocking the hammer, "Go ahead. Make my day."

Trembling, the young man managed to pick the Queen of Hearts. He shuffled the deck and handed it back to the President.

"Think you've got the hang of it yet?" the President asked, cutting the deck several times. "Well, I hope so, because this," he said, holding up the Six of Diamonds, "is your card."

The young man sat stunned for a second before he exclaimed: "Amazing!" grinning and nodding furiously. "How did you do that?"

"Practice," the President smiled, "and a whole lot of wishing. Of course, it certainly helps when you're able to flex your muscles and get off a few good rounds now and then, but there's always ample opportunity for that sort of thing," and the President returned the gun to his suit pocket. "How are you feeling?" he asked.

"A little nauseous," said the young man, "but it's an enlightened nausea."

"Good, good," the President said. "Explaining why **One Minute Retaliations** work has always been an exhilarating experience for me, second only to an actual retaliation itself. As for the thrill of being on the receiving end of a **One Minute Retaliation**, well, you can put that in your own words."

"I'd rather not."

"Well put," said the President. "But you have to admit it's one hell of a pretense."

"It certainly is," the young man admitted.

"Look at it this way," the President smiled, "If you can threaten enough people with force rather than words, you can eventually end up doing anything you want any time, any place, and for any reason. And when you can do whatever you want, you can say whatever you want. It's virtually endless."

"I believe you," the young man shrugged, "You've got the gun."

"That's right," the President continued, "but it's more than just having the gun. The major problem in the world today is the same as it's ever been. Nobody wants to die. Take me. I'm certainly not getting any younger, although I wouldn't bet against it. But every weekend I fly to the ranch to chop wood and ride horses and rope a few doggies just so I can keep on living. Why do you think I do this?"

"Because the country would be lost without you?"

"Not bad," said the President, "but there are those who claim the only reason anyone keeps himself alive is that death doesn't seem particularly interesting. Even Mark Twain used to say that if the good life in heaven is like the good life here on earth, who needs it?

"What's more," the President continued, "some people think existence is absurd, that life is meaningless, and death is what makes it meaningless, so they continue to live in order to give their lives some meaning. Other people think life is an initiation ritual to prepare the chosen for the promised land, so they continue to suffer as long as they can so they'll be assured the best seats at that great Beach Boys concert in the sky. But most people stay alive because they simply don't have enough guts to kill themselves."

"I never heard it put that way before," the young man said, nodding his head, "but it makes perfectly good sense, hearing you say it."

"Of course you didn't, and of course it does," said the President, "and today the situation is even graver than we suspect. Do you realize that there are nearly four billion people on this planet that really need to kill themselves but don't have what it takes to do the job?"

"I had no idea."

"Well, it's true," said the President, "Here. Take a look at this," and he pulled the familiar device from his pocket, and another Presidential aphorism appeared on the screen.

There Are Just Two Kinds Of People

In The World

If We Don't Count You

"If you remember that you are in charge, and not merely an elected official," the President concluded, "you'll do okay."

"That doesn't seem to follow," the young man said.

"I'm pleased to see you got my message, young man. You will have success with the **One Minute Retaliation** only after you have mastered the POF Principle and the habit of self-enrichment."

"Yes, of course I will, and of course I must," the young man butted in, "But that reminds me, I've made up a little saying of my own to remind me how **Wishes**, and their consequences—**Gladhands** and **Retaliations**—can help me get what I want in the shortest possible time."

How Sleep The Brave

Who Sink To Rest

By All Their Country's

Wishes Blessed

"That's very good!" the President exclaimed.

"Do you really think so?" the young man asked, not wanting to admit he had copied the words from a third-grade silent reader he'd found in a used-book store the evening before.

"Young man," the President said very slowly, tapping his suit pocket for emphasis, "would you like to play the game again?"

Just when he thought he would get **Gladhanded**, the young man felt he was in for another **Retaliation**, something he would really rather avoid.

"Do I have to?"

"No question about it," the President said. "But not today," he winked, and the young man thought he might wet himself he was so relieved.

"You know, young man," the President continued, turning to stare at his favorite blank wall, "You've demonstrated for me a certain flair for words on several occasions, although I can't now name the first one. And I should know."

"You certainly should."

"And since I like you, I'm willing to stick part of my neck out for you," the President said, still staring at the wall. "How would you like to become one of my speech-writers?"

The young man put down his notebook and gaped in astonishment at the President's back. "You mean and go to work for the nicest guy anyone would ever want to meet?"

"It's a foot in the door," said the President.

"And all I've got to do is keep on doing whatever it is I'm doing?"

"Like the rest of the team."

This was, of course, what the young man had been searching for all his life. He was overcome by the moment. "I...I don't know what to say," he finally said.

"Spoken like a real trouper," the **One Minute President** said, without turning around. "And for someone who's just been hired to put words in my mouth, I'd say you're already showing great promise." And with that, the President produced his device and clicked it three times.

Suddenly, the office went completely black, and the young man found himself sitting in the sofa chair feeling strangely alone. Everything was so dark and quiet that he momentarily wondered if he hadn't suffered a stroke.

But this lasted no more than a few seconds, for, just as suddenly, the huge video screen burst alive, illuminating the office in white light. There, up on the screen in front of him was the enormous face of the **One Minute President**, dwarfing the young man's presence like a front-row moviegoer whose eyes have been permanently wired open.

"Welcome aboard," smiled the image of the President.

And the young man proudly smiled back. "It's an honor, sir. I'm thrilled."

"Of course it is, and of course you are," the President's image agreed. "And until we meet again —if ever—this is goodbye and *auf wiedersehen.*"

"But..."

"No more ifs, ands, buts or maybes, young man," the President said, tapping his suit pocket for emphasis. "This is it."

And so it was—until the old geezer died.

But what little time the special President had invested in the young man paid off. Because eventually, as happens in so many American fairy tales, the inevitable happened.

 HE BECAME A One Minute President.

He became a **One Minute President** not because he thought like one, but because he pretended it was the only way to live.

He made **One Minute Wishes.**

He gave **One Minute Gladhands.**

He indulged in **One Minute Retaliations.**

He asked brief, evasive questions; stared at the blank wall in his uncluttered office for days at a time; followed the POF Principle; laughed, played, and told the rest of the world where to get off.

And, perhaps most important of all, he encouraged the people he worked with or ruled to keep on doing whatever they were doing.

He had even created a pocket size "Game Plan" to make it easier for the people who worked for him to become **One Minute Presidents** themselves. He had sold it at a substantial discount to each of the two million people who reported to him.

A very brief summary of

THE ONE MINUTE PRESIDENT'S "GAMEPLAN"

How to give yourself & others "The Tip"
to getting whatever you want whenever you want it

MAKE WISHES; GLADHAND AND RETALIATE; SACRIFICE PEOPLE;
SAY WHATEVER YOU WANT; LAUGH; VACATION; SHIFT BLAME
and encourage the people you rule to do the same as you!

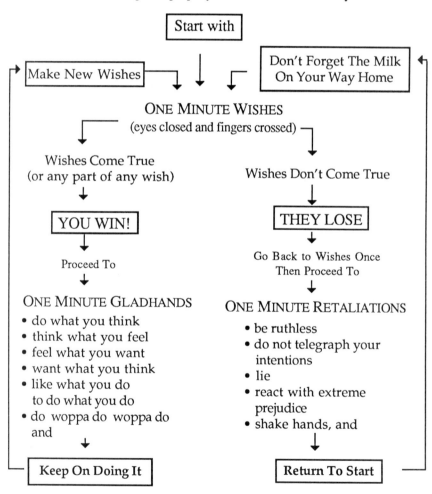

MANY YEARS LATER, the man looked back on the time when he first heard of the principles of **One Minute Presidenting**. It seemed like ages ago. He was glad he had written down what he learned from the **One Minute President**. His notes had become a best-seller at $25 a copy.

By selling copies of his book to many other people he had assured that he wouldn't have to work as hard as he grew older simply to stay alive. He would have time to chop wood and ride horses and take trips to threaten important people in other countries. He would advise future Presidents how to best fulfill their wishes by shaking the right hands and cutting off all the others.

Everyone who worked for him felt secure. No one felt manipulated or threatened because everyone knew from the start that no one knew what he was doing or why.

Many of the people reporting to him had become **One Minute Presidents** in obscure emerging nations themselves. And they, in turn, had done the same for many of the people who reported to them.

The entire universe had become more effective.

And with a little luck, they might all live forever...

 SUDDENLY HE HEARD SOMEONE clear his throat at the door.

"Come in, come in," he said, striding across to the door to acknowledge the arrival of a bright and inquisitive young man, "I've been expecting you."

The new **One Minute President** was very pleased, and he was surprised at how pleased he was. In many ways, this visitor reminded him of someone he knew long ago, if he could only put his finger on his name, and this thought made him young again.

"I want to have a deep and meaningful relationship with you," he heard himself telling the young man, "Have a seat."

Afterwards, while they were washing up, he found himself as comfortable and glib in talking with this bright young man as the old geezer had once been with him. "I'll be happy to engage in these casual encounters and to share with you an occasional secret," the new **One Minute President** told his handsome visitor, as he led him back to the sofa-chair. "I will make only one request."

"What is that?" his protege asked.

"Simply," the President began, "that you…

Don't Remember

Any Of This

About The Perpetrators

PAUL FERICANO AND ELIO LIGI are literary extremists whose satires and hoaxes have angered the mighty and amused the powerless for nearly three decades.

Their activities and attitudes are so controversial they were ousted from Terrorist Poets & Writers in 1984 for, among other things, the pie bombing of an Adrienne Rich reading and an aborted attempt to hijack the Olympic Torch in Selma, Alabama.

Shortly thereafter, they founded Yossarian Universal News Service, Earth's first and only international parody news and disinformation service.

Fericano lives in California with his wife, Kathy, and their daughter, Kate.

Ligi was last photographed in Moammar Qadaffi's supreme mess tent, preparing the liver of a former Minister of Finance for Field Marshall and President for Life Idi Amin Dada, VC, DSO, and Commander-In-Chief of the Ugandan Armed Forces.